RESTORATION
FORCE

RESTORATION
FORCE

GRASS ROOTS PRESERVATION OF CIVILIAN AND
MILITARY AIRCRAFT BY ENTHUSIASTS WORLDWIDE

GAVIN HOFFEN

GRUB STREET • LONDON

Title page photograph: A Harrier AV-8B outside her home in snowy conditions.*

Front cover photograph: Buccaneer XX899 at Newark Air Museum in 2018.
(Keith Campbell)

Back cover photographs. From top to bottom:

Who needs sweeping views of the countryside when you have a Harrier parked outside?

The fuselage of Firefly WD889 which was constructed as a Firefly AS.6; an anti-submarine aircraft that carried British equipment.

De Havilland Sea Venom FAW.22 XG692 cockpit section taken at her home in South Manchester.

A very rare British Airways BAC 1-11 510ED simulator.

*NB: The author refers to aircraft, cockpits and bits thereof as 'her' throughout the book.

Published by
Grub Street
4 Rainham Close
London SW11 6SS

A CIP record for this title is available from the British library

ISBN-13: 978-1-911667-13-1

Design by Lucy Thorne

Printed and bound by Finidr in the Czech Republic

CONTENTS

ACKNOWLEDGEMENTS

First and foremost, I would like to thank wholeheartedly the kind people who took the time to share with me their projects and their incredible knowledge. It has been a great experience and learning curve working with them all. To the photographers, who kindly allowed me to use their historical photographs, and for all of their kind words of encouragement during the writing process. To Keith Campbell from 'Capture A Second' for allowing me to use his amazing photograph that serves as the front cover. A special thanks to Tony Clay, the webmaster for 74 Squadron for putting up with my pestering and tracking down Tony Dixon (the person who took the photograph of the 74 Squadron Phantom in Chapter Six). Dave Taylor deserves a special mention. Not only did he sell me Chipmunk WK638, but as the fountain of all knowledge when it comes to cockpits and the people who own them, he was always there on hand to guide me in the right direction. If anybody is thinking of entering into this unique hobby, then Dave Taylor should be your first port of call. He can be found on the 'Aircraft cockpit & instrument panel collectors' Facebook group. Last but certainly not least, to Loz, for all of her patience and encouragement.

INTRODUCTION

It is very true that we can all walk into any of the many aircraft museums around the world and appreciate the wonderfully restored and preserved exhibits on display. But with this book, I wanted the reader to discover the many gems that are hiding away in people's garages, sheds, barns and gardens that are generally not accessible to the general public.

I must admit that writing this book became far more challenging than I had first anticipated. I was naive when I first set out on this journey thinking that everybody would want their beloved projects featured in a new publication detailing their hard work and efforts, but it soon became apparent that this would not always be the case. To outsiders of this 'hobby' it can be difficult to understand, but to a 'cockpiteer' their project that is lovingly kept safe away from harm is more precious and sentimental to them than say, having the last Ferrari F1 car that Michael Schumacher ever drove sat in their garage. They really are that precious to them. For this reason, I wholeheartedly thank everybody who has contributed to making this book possible and allowing me into their world. So as not to jeopardise the security of these projects, names and locations have been limited to the very basics.

When I first conceived the concept of this book, the most common question friends and family would ask me was 'why?' Why try and attempt to write a book about aircraft that can no longer fly, or that are not even housed in a museum? For those without the 'bug' it is completely alien to them to understand why someone would want to dedicate so much time, effort, and money into something that is quite literally an obsession. For myself, it all started becoming real one Saturday morning (after spending the previous evening at the local pub) with the realisation that I had successfully bid on an aircraft cockpit on eBay. Not wanting to renege from my formal agreement to purchase the item, even though I had no memory of making the bid, I arranged to hire a van and set off on a long journey to pick up my new acquisition. After spending nearly an entire day on the road, I was fortunate enough on my return to realise that the cockpit fitted (only by a whisker) into my garage. I clearly had not prepared properly for this venture. I did what most people do with their cockpits and aircraft and set up her own little dedicated Facebook page detailing photographs of her when she was in service and regular

Chipmunk WK638 'Hilda' photo taken in 2010.

updates on any progress that was made on any given day. My valuable free time was now being used to scour the internet for missing parts needed to complete the project. To my sheer delight, it was only a matter of weeks before a farmer contacted me from the north of England to tell me that he had in his possession the rear fuselage of my plane; my project and obsession was growing and in memory of my grandmother who had passed away around that time, I christened my aircraft 'Hilda'.

After several years, a relocation and a new property purchase on a house without a garage, my hand was forced in relinquishing tenureship of my Chipmunk and handing over the custodianship to somebody else. Many years had passed, but still feeling seller's remorse, I cannot explain the sheer delight I felt when the new custodian of WK638 responded to my request for material for this book. We will meet Hilda a bit later on.

With modern-day aviation heading in the direction that it is today, pilotless drones and futuristic flying computers, I fear that we are in danger of losing the romantic nostalgia that aviation once was. I am in my late thirties now (fast approaching forty) and I can still remember as a young boy growing up in a Wiltshire village, a local farmer who used an old Spitfire bubble canopy on his allotment to keep his vegetables out of harm's way, and a leather headrest also from a Spitfire attached to his tractor. It is this spirit of grassroots preservation that I hope *Restoration Force* goes some way in celebrating as it does the dedication of all the people who have contributed in making this publication possible.

The photographs have been provided by the owners of the featured projects, or by photographers whose photographs feature the aircraft in active service. (NB: All photos are copyrighted to the owners except where stated.) As many of the aircraft are older than me, the quality of the photographs may not be quite to the standard of today's modern cameras. You will discover that some chapters are more detailed and longer than others, this is purely down to the information and photographs available and does not reflect the significance or importance of any given project. All the information relating to the histories of each featured aircraft has kindly been supplied by the contributor of the project, and I therefore apologise if there are any inaccuracies. It has been a conscious decision not to give too much of a detailed description of each aircraft type as I am fully aware that most folk reading this will be fully fledged experts in aviation, but for those who don't know what an Avro Vulcan is fear not, for you will find a brief description of each aircraft type featured in the book. Lastly, if you have always dreamt about owning your very own piece of aviation, or have ever aspired to having your very own garden air force then you will discover how other such enthusiasts have gone about achieving this within the chapters herein.

I hope you enjoy reading this book as much as I have enjoyed piecing it together.

1 MATTHEW
FROM CAMBRIDGESHIRE

The English Electric Lightning was capable of flying twice the speed of sound and was the only all-British supersonic fighter to have been used by the Royal Air Force. Conceived to stand up against the threat of the Soviet Union during the Cold War, her incredible climb rate and operating ceiling of over 60,000 feet made the Lightning perfect for intercepting long-range Soviet reconnaissance and bomber aircraft.

Having operated as a front-line interceptor for 34 years, it is remarkable to consider that the Lightning did not record one single kill during her operational duties. In total 337 Lightnings were produced and they would go on to serve not only with the RAF but with the Royal Saudi Air Force and the Kuwait Air Force before retirement in the late 1980s. Although only an exceedingly small number of Lightnings fly today, there are numerous static airframes in museums all around the world. With over 30 years having passed since retirement, the Lightning remains a firm favourite with aviation enthusiasts around the globe.

For those wondering what the first thing is that you need to become an owner of a fast-jet cockpit (apart from deep pockets and a place to store it), Matthew has the answer: "You have to have a very understanding wife to

Lightning XR754 taken at RAF Mildenhall Air Fete in May 1988. (Derek Heley)

Matthew's Lightning XR754 in his back garden in Cambridgeshire.

have the nose of a Lightning in the garden."

XR754's first flight was on 8 July 1965 and she would go on to serve with 5 Squadron, 23 Squadron and then onto 11 Squadron. In September 1984 she suffered an engine fire at Souda Bay on the Greek island of Crete whilst returning from armament practice camp at RAF Akrotiri in Cyprus. When she finally returned home to RAF Binbrook, she was adorned with the shark's mouth markings on her nose. In May 1988 she was allotted to RAF Honington as a ground instructional airframe. After 3,893 flying hours she was eventually broken up for scrap and taken to Hanningfield Metals in Chelmsford, Essex, in February 1992. The cockpit section would

This photograph taken in November 2013 shows the extent of the restoration works required when Matthew took ownership.

The Lightning on the road on her way to Cambridgeshire in 2013.

pass through the hands of several aviation museums before Matthew purchased her in November 2013.

Before Matthew's Lightning would go on to become an award-winning exhibit at Cockpitfest (a two-day event held at Newark Air Museum that attracts exhibitors with cockpits and other aircraft artefacts from the UK and Europe), winning the Spirit of Cockpitfest in 2015, he had a mountain to climb in bringing the cockpit back to the condition it was in when she retired in the late 1980s. XR754 became not only a labour of love for Matthew but also became a member of his family.

When Matthew picked up the Lightning from Doncaster Air Museum, which had been her long-term home, she was in a good overall solid condition with all frames in place inside the cockpit (albeit missing most of the instrumentation). When she was scrapped at Hanningfield Metals, the nose section was removed from the wrong side of the transport joint leaving quite a mess, meaning Matthew would have to rebuild and tidy up 754's spine. She was still wearing her grey paint scheme that she acquired in January 1983 when Matthew took ownership of her, and although it had stood the test of time well, it was missing its RAF markings and decals. After a few years and some extensive research, Matthew added the markings and the decals to the original paintwork to add to the overall impression of the cockpit section.

Matthew with his wife, Beccy and three children at Newark in 2019.

XR754 now adorning RAF markings, ejector seat decals and the shark's mouth that represents her tour to Cyprus with 5 Squadron in 1984. You can also see the tail fin of 754 which Matthew purchased from an auction about three years ago.

The lightning bolt on the side of XR754 represents her time with 11 Squadron in 1988 with Ian Black (one of the last Lightning pilots, serving with 11 Squadron) closing the Mildenhall Air Fete in May 1988.

Inside the cockpit of XR754 showing the great work that Matthew has done to date.

When the quick reaction alert (QRA) shed was taken down at RAF Wattisham and re-erected at RAF Bruntingthorpe in 2014, a grand opening was held attended by many Lightning exhibits. Here XR754 looks completely at home.

XR754 on display at Shuttleworth in 2018.

On display at Cockpitfest, Newark, in 2019.

Avro Vulcan XA903 carrying the Blue Steel nuclear missile taken in 1960. (Mike Dowsing)

2 STEVE
FROM STONEYKIRK

The Avro Vulcan entered service with the Royal Air Force in 1956 as part of the country's airborne nuclear deterrent during the height of the Cold War. Designed primarily to carry nuclear weapons, the Vulcan was also capable of carrying a conventional bomb load, a task that she successfully carried out during the Falklands War participating in the much-celebrated Black Buck operation. The Royal Air Force retired the Vulcan in 1984, and although the iconic aircraft would no longer serve in an active capacity, one Vulcan, XH558 would continue to thrill air show crowds up until as recently as 2015 when the last flying Vulcan was grounded due to mounting maintenance costs and lack of surplus spares to keep the aircraft in the sky.

To say that Steve's collection is impressive is somewhat of an understatement. You would be forgiven for thinking that this was a mainstream museum, but it is in fact a private collection housed in his barn, although visitors are welcome by prior arrangement.

The view from inside Steve's barn that is home to six fully restored cockpit sections.

Perhaps the star of the show is Steve's Avro Vulcan cockpit section, which is one of only two forward sections of a MK1 Vulcan remaining. XA903 was the only MK1 Vulcan to carry the Blue Steel stand-off missile (part of the United Kingdom's nuclear deterrent) and did so to test the missile and the Vulcan's ability to use it. She was used as a flying testbed for the Concorde Olympus engines and performed extensive testing of the engine prior to Concorde flying. After her last flight, 903 survived for some time at Farnborough becoming more decrepit until she was finally scrapped. She passed through the hands of several Vulcan enthusiasts before being acquired by Steve. Steve, being the perfectionist that he is, brought the aircraft to his residence in Scotland and set about bringing her back to her former glory days.

Inside the cockpit of XA903.

Another one of Steve's impressive exhibits is the cockpit section of Canberra WE191. The Canberra was a high-altitude and high-speed jet-powered medium bomber that set a world altitude

record of over 70,000 ft in 1957. The Royal Air Force retired its Canberra fleet in 2006 having been in service with them for over 50 years.

Built in 1954, WE191 flew with the following Royal Air Force units: 231 Operational Conversion Unit (OCU), 237 OCU and 54 Squadron. She was then converted for sale to the Indian Air Force, but the sale did not proceed; the aircraft was eventually sold to the British Aircraft Corporation in 1978. She remained in storage until purchased by Dumfries Aviation Museum in 2001. Steve purchased the nose section from the museum in 2012.

XA903 painted in its original white 'anti-flash' colour scheme designed to reflect some of the thermal radiation from a nuclear explosion. In later years, the Vulcan would take on a more familiar grey and green camouflage scheme.

The nose section of Canberra WE191

Another aircraft in Steve's collection is the de Havilland Vampire which was the first-ever jet fighter aircraft to be powered by a single jet engine. She entered service with the Royal Air Force only months after the end of World War Two. Having carried out several different roles for the RAF, the Vampire was eventually retired from her last role as an advanced training aircraft in 1966.

Vampire T-11 XE921 was constructed in 1955 and entered service with the Royal Air Force on 7 March of that year. She spent seven years with the Central Flying School at RAF Little Rissington from 1956 to 1963. In 1971 the front fuselage was sold to Exeter airport. She passed through several private collector's hands before Steve acquired her and started work on the renovation to get her back to the condition she is in today.

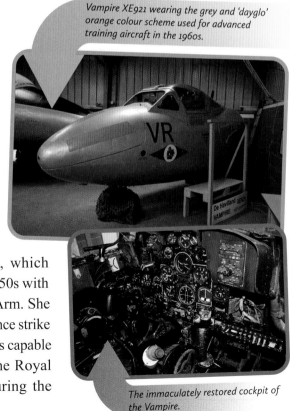
Vampire XE921 wearing the grey and 'dayglo' orange colour scheme used for advanced training aircraft in the 1960s.

The immaculately restored cockpit of the Vampire.

Yet another of Steve's projects is the Sea Vixen, which entered service in the late 1950s with the Royal Navy's Fleet Air Arm. She was a carrier-based fleet defence strike fighter which replaced the less capable Sea Venom. Flying from the Royal Navy's aircraft carriers during the

Sea Vixen XP925 taken at Royal Navy Air Service (RNAS) Yeovilton in 1972. (Chris England)

XP925 restored and safely preserved in Steve's barn.

Hawker Sea Hawk WV903 taken at RNAS Culdrose in 1981. (John Bolt and Peter Davis)

height of the Cold War, this twin turbojet fighter was the first British aircraft to carry guided missiles, rockets and bombs making her a formidable force in protecting the nation's naval fleet. Later variants of the Sea Vixen would see modifications such as foldable wing tips and nose cone making storage on the cramped aircraft carriers much easier. All in all, a total of 145 Sea Vixens were built before their retirement in 1972. Out of those built, one in three were lost to accidents. The last flying Sea Vixen, 'Foxy Lady', suffered undercarriage failure after a display at Duxford Air Show in 2017. It is estimated that it will take four years' worth of work and three million pounds to get the aircraft back in the sky again.

XP925 had a hard life after retirement from the Fleet Air Arm. She was donated to the Air Training Corps by the Defence Research Agency based at Farnborough in 1994. She had spent several years on the airfield's fire pit and by the time she was donated to the ATC she was nothing more than a gutted shell. Over the following years a group of enthusiasts formed the Sea Vixen Preservation Group and work commenced on the restoration of this rare war bird.

Steve also has a Sea Hawk! First introduced in the mid-1950s, over 500 of the single-seat jet-powered fighters were manufactured. Capable of flying from naval aircraft carriers, the Hawker Sea Hawk was operated by the Royal Navy's Fleet Air Arm, the Indian navy, the Dutch navy, and the German navy. Although the Sea Hawk proved herself to be a reliable workhorse, her operational life turned out to be relatively short. With the introduction of the more powerful and heavily armed Sea Vixen, the Sea Hawks started to be phased out from the Fleet Air Arm in 1958.

Steve's Sea Hawk, WV903, entered service in 1954 and served with 804, 811, 897 and 802 Naval Air Squadrons. Her last active flying duties were with 801 Naval Air Squadron before she was retired from front-line duties in 1961. Having been acquired by several instructional training establishments she eventually found herself at the School of Aircraft Handling at RNAS Culdrose in 1976 where she would remain until 1985. She would spend nine years in storage at RNAS Lee-on-Solent in Hampshire before being put up for disposal in 1994. She was moved to RNAS Yeovilton in 1995 and remained in open store for several years.

By 2007, WV903 was now in the hands of a private enthusiast, but

The cockpit section of Sea Hawk WV903 looking as it did when she entered service in 1954.

The fully restored cockpit section of Jet Provost XP558.

The nose section of XP558 wearing the Macaw on the side of her fuselage from the MACAWS display team (MAnby College of Air Warfare).

unfortunately her wings by this time had not escaped the fate of the scrapyard. In 2015 she changed hands again and was delivered to Steve in Scotland where she remains to this day.

Finally, the Jet Provost which began service with the Royal Air Force in the late 1950s and was employed as their primary two-seat jet-powered trainer. Later variants would see a more powerful engine and a pressurised cockpit which would enable the RAF to use the aircraft in several different roles including aerobatics, tactical weapons training and advanced training. A light ground-attack variant was produced, employed by several air forces across the world and renamed the Strikemaster. The Jet Provost was eventually retired in the 1990s, but the reliability, easy maintenance and relatively low operating costs made her a firm favourite with enthusiast and private operators alike.

XP558 is a MK4 Jet Provost and was manufactured in 1962, spending her initial life at RAF Cranfield. She later moved to RAF Manby College of Air Warfare where she flew as part of the MACAWS display team. After her time at Manby, she was moved to RNAS Culdrose to be used as an 'instructional' aircraft. Following retirement from the RAF, she was acquired by a flight simulator enthusiast who had the cockpit section removed prior to being converted into a sim. She was eventually sold, which is when Steve started the long journey in restoring her back to her formal glory days.

3 ROBIN
FROM OXFORDSHIRE

Robin's collection encompasses a Buccaneer, a Fairey Gannet and a Sea Vixen.

Initially conceived for the Royal Navy, the Buccaneer was designed for low-level operations over land and sea. Entering service with the Royal Navy in July 1962, it soon became apparent that the MK1 Buccaneers lacked serious power when taking off from the aircraft carriers with a full weapon load and fuel tank. Clearly the procedure of taking off with a reduced fuel load and having to 'top up' immediately using the soon-to-be redundant Scimitars was not going to suffice. These issues were remedied with the improved, more powerful Buccaneer S.2s. After the Labour government cancelled the TSR-2 programme, the RAF were reluctant to employ an aircraft designed for the Royal Navy, but with a big hole to fill, the Buccaneer entered service with the RAF in 1969. She would go on to thrive with the RAF and proved her weight in gold during the first Gulf War. There the aging Buccaneers designated targets for the Tornado-delivered laser-guided bombs as well as carrying out sorties dropping LGBs themselves. Unlike the Tornado, the Buccaneer did not suffer a loss during the conflict. A few years after the war, the last of the Buccaneers was finally retired from service in 1994.

Robin's Buccaneer cockpit section has been removed from the fuse-lage further back from the cockpit than most cockpit sections in order for the canopy to be able to slide open on its rails. Seen here at the Midland Air Museum.

Robin has had an interest in aviation ever since he was a small boy having started going to air shows in the late 1970s. The one aircraft that would always catch his eye was the Buccaneer as it was so different from other aircraft of that era. He then developed a huge interest in aircraft of the 1950s, 1960s and 1970s and in particular the Sea Vixen and aircraft of the Fleet Air Arm. When the Buccaneer fleet was retired, Robin was fortunate enough to know the gentleman at Hanningfield Metals who had bought most of the last aircraft that flew down to St Athan to be scrapped. When Robin visited the yard, he found the fuselage of XX899 there waiting her turn. Others had already been sold as complete airframes, along with several Phantoms being scrapped. This Buccaneer was the last one left. Steve from Hanningfield Metals offered to sell Robin the cockpit section, and after a lot of consideration, he could not resist the opportunity actually to own part of his favourite aircraft. Fortunately, there was enough room at the car body shop where Robin worked at the time for the cockpit to be kept there. He counts himself lucky that he was able to see 899 as a complete fuselage giving him the chance to have the cockpit section cut behind the canopy rail and engine cowling, so enabling the canopy to be wound right back correctly (all other Buccaneer cockpits are cut behind the canopy, making it difficult to open correctly).

Robin also considers himself to be very fortunate to have been given the chance to own 899 as she had just come out of service and the front cockpit was about 75 per cent complete. The rear cockpit however had not fared so well as many of the instruments had been recovered for spares and the radar was also missing from the nose. Robin has spent the last 20-odd years sourcing the missing parts and now has everything apart from one instrument for the rear cockpit. Several years ago, Robin started a full repaint as she was looking a bit tired, however progress has been slightly slower than

The now complete and fully restored front cockpit.

anticipated due to long-term health problems; she is now at Newark, and he is hoping to have the full restoration complete this year.

Buccaneer XX899 entered service in September 1976 having been delivered to 12 Squadron at RAF Honington. A transfer four years later to 208 Squadron would see her remain at Honington for one month when an overseas posting to 15 Squadron would see her move to Germany to her new base, RAF Laarbruch. Four years later, having moved to 16 Squadron, she would be back at Honington for seven months with 237 Operational Conversion Unit. A move to north-east Scotland next when 237 OCU relocated to RAF Lossiemouth in October 1984. A transfer back to 12 Squadron would see her stay at Lossiemouth until conflict descended on the Middle East.

In January 1991 she was prepared for Operation Granby having been painted in desert 'pink'. On 26 January of the same year, she was the first of six Buccaneers to fly direct to Muharraq Air Base in Bahrain taking 8.5 hours with inflight refuelling. In February 1991, she was the lead Buccaneer with Buccaneer XW547 and four Tornados on a mission to take out the As Samawah road and bridge. Nose art 'Laser Lips Laura' was added later on in the campaign and 19 mission symbols displayed below the starboard windscreen.

She returned to RAF Lossiemouth, re-joining 12 Squadron in March 1991. Her desert art had been removed by the June of that year. In October 1993,

Buccaneer XX899 wearing her 'Laser Lips Laura' artwork and desert 'pink' colour scheme. Taken in Bahrain in March 1991. (Nick Weight)

12 Squadron had disbanded and XX899 transferred to 208 Squadron retaining her 12 Squadron markings. Now nearing the end of her career, she performed the public solo flying display at the Buccaneer retirement celebration at RAF Lossiemouth in March 1994. She would make her last flight on 6 April 1994, flying from RAF Lossiemouth to RAF St Athan where she was stored and partially scrapped having flown a total of 4235.15 flying hours. In October, the aircraft was scrapped, and the remains sent to Hanningfield Metals.

With tensions rising between the Soviet Union and the West in the 1950s, allied navies started to focus their attentions on the growing Soviet submarine fleet. A carrier-based aircraft was required to boost surveillance operations and be capable of anti-submarine warfare. The twin-turboprop Fairey Gannet entered service in 1953 and would serve not only with the Royal Navy's Fleet Air Arm but also with the German navy and the Royal Australian Navy. By the mid-1960s the Royal Navy's anti-submarine Gannets started to be replaced by the Westland Whirlwind. The remaining Gannets would remain in service for another decade carrying out various other roles before the fleet was eventually retired in the late 1970s.

Fairey Gannet XL449 made her first flight from White Waltham in December 1958. From 1958 to 1962 she was fairly transient having spells at Boscombe Down, White Waltham, HMS *Victorious* and RAE Bedford before postings to the Aircraft Handling Flight at RNAS Culdrose and 849 Squadron HQ Flight in August 1962. 1963 would see moves to RNAS Lossiemouth, Westland White Waltham and Westland Ilchester. After she had undergone repairs and modifications in May 1965, by the December she was at the Naval Aircraft Support Unit at RNAS Brawdy. She would spend most of 1966 and 1967 with 849 Squadron HQ Flight, coded 763/BY. By December 1967 she was with 849 Squadron A Flight at RNAS Brawdy then aboard HMS *Hermes*. A year later she was with D Flight of 849 Squadron at RNAS Brawdy then seabound again aboard HMS *Eagle*. By August 1969 she was back at RNAS Brawdy with 849 HQ Flight. In September 1970 she was back at RNAS Lossiemouth with the Gannet Support Flight where she would spend the next three years. After a stint with 849 B flight at Lossiemouth she would be back at sea aboard HMS *Ark Royal*.

After four years back with 849 HQ Flight she would move to the Aircraft Handling Unit at RNAS Lossiemouth and struck off charge in June 1978.

A very sad looking XX899 at Hanningfield Metals in 1994. A tail of a Tiger Squadron Phantom can be seen in the background. (Mark Jones)

XX899 looking stunning, taken at Newark Air Museum in 2018. The photographer who took this takes some incredible aviation photographs. For more information visit www.capture-asecond.com. (Keith Campbell)

Fairey Gannet XL449 taken at the South Wales Aircraft Museum, Cardiff in September 1985. (Kev Slade)

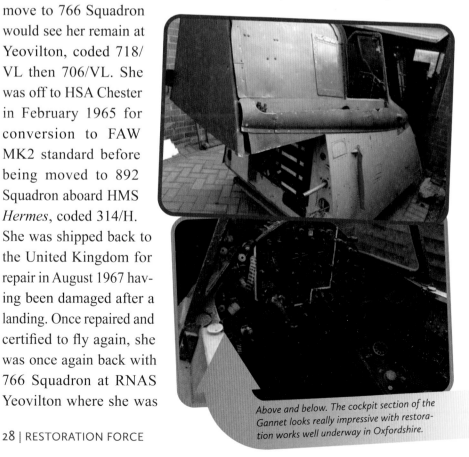

Fairey Gannet XL449 cockpit section on Robin's driveway in Oxfordshire.

In the same year she was moved to SWAM at Rhoose Airport in Cardiff where she would remain for eight years until the aircraft was broken up on site and the cockpit section passed through the hands of a couple of aircraft enthusiasts. In August 2015 Robin acquired the cockpit from Parkhouse Aviation and transported her back to his home in Oxfordshire.

Robin is desperately looking for a canopy, please get in touch if you know of one for sale!

Built as FAW MK1 in late 1960/early 1961, Sea Vixen XN647 took her first flight in January 1961 before she was posted to 899 Squadron at RNAS Yeovilton in April 1962, coded 490/VL. Two years later, in May 1964, a move to 766 Squadron would see her remain at Yeovilton, coded 718/VL then 706/VL. She was off to HSA Chester in February 1965 for conversion to FAW MK2 standard before being moved to 892 Squadron aboard HMS *Hermes*, coded 314/H. She was shipped back to the United Kingdom for repair in August 1967 having been damaged after a landing. Once repaired and certified to fly again, she was once again back with 766 Squadron at RNAS Yeovilton where she was

Above and below. The cockpit section of the Gannet looks really impressive with restoration works well underway in Oxfordshire.

coded 707/YL. In July 1970 she was damaged again and moved by road to RNAS Culdrose to be used as a ground instruction airframe coded SAH-10 and then SAH-11, final flying hours 1787.50. By mid-1978 she was towed to Corn-

De Havilland Sea Vixen XN647 taken at RAF Chivenor in August 1970. (Stephen Rendle)

wall Aero Park and put on display where she would remain for over 20 years. In early 2000, she was scrapped and moved to Bruntingthorpe.

Robin has always had a soft spot for the Sea Vixen being unusual and so typically British, so when he heard that a gentleman called Nev Martin had the remains of Sea Vixen XN647 in his yard, Robin couldn't resist and

had to have her. Unfortunately, after many years of neglect she was in a bit of a sorry state with everything inside water damaged and the outside badly faded and damaged. It has taken Robin several years to clean, restore and replace everything, including the windscreens, and to fully restore and respray the panel work (being a trained car bodywork specialist helped). The Vixen is now 80 per cent finished with just some internal work required to be completed.

XN647 back in 2004 clearly in need of some attention after being scrapped at Bruntingthorpe.

After Robin's hard work the Sea Vixen now looks as good as when she took her first flight back in 1961.

Jaguar XX720 taken at RAF Coltishall in June 2000. (Kev Slade)

4 GED
FROM KENT

The Sepecat Jaguar was the final product from a joint venture between the French and the British and would serve in the air forces of both countries as well as the Indian Air Force. Making its first flight in 1968, the Jaguar entered service in 1973 and would enjoy a long career before being retired by the French in 2005 and 2007 by the United Kingdom. Originally designed for training purposes with the capability to perform light ground-attack roles, it soon became apparent that the Jaguar would need to be able to perform a more aggressive role. The result would see the Jaguar capable of supersonic flight and of carrying a nuclear payload. The Jaguar would see combat in several conflicts including operations during the 1991 Gulf War.

Jaguar XX720 first flew on 16 April 1974 and was delivered to the Royal Air Force in May of that year. She would spend most of her service life flying with 54(F) Squadron, a strike fighter unit which at the time was operating from RAF Coltishall in Norfolk.

For Ged from Kent, his passion was awakened by owning a replica Spitfire, and although perhaps one of the most iconic aircraft in existence to this day, he found that he was wanting a project that was more demanding. In the true spirit of Restoration Force Ged, his brother Les and mutual good friend Chris, while working on the Spitfire wing one Sunday morning had

An aerial drone shot of Ged's garden after the arrival of his two aircraft.

the mad idea of owning a Harrier Jump Jet. After a brief internet search and a number of telephone calls later, the trio purchased not one, but two jets in 2018 from Everett Aero in Ipswich. A Jaguar GR3 and a Harrier AV-8B.

Moving the aircraft from Ipswich to Kent was no easy feat. Each aircraft required two low loaders, one to carry the fuselage and the other to trans-

port the wings. Then heavy-lifting machinery was needed to lift all the components into place. Fortunately, the trio managed to source a lot of new, old stock and second-hand parts to get the aircraft back to their former glory.

The trio's Harrier is an AV-8B that served with the United States Marine Corps. In October 1988

Although XX720 was relatively complete when Ged took ownership, there is still a small number of panels that are required to complete her.

she was delivered to Marine Attack Squadron VMA-311 known as the 'Tom-cats'. In December of the same year, she was transferred to Marine Attack Squadron VMA-513 who go by the name of the 'Flying Nightmares'. It was with this squadron that she was deployed in 1991 for operations in Desert Storm and Desert Shield (although it is not clear if she participated in active combat missions during the conflict). In 1993 the aircraft was transferred to the 'Wake Island Avengers' also known as Marine Attack Squadron VMA-211. She was finally retired from service in November 1997. It seems the fuselage was imported by the Ministry of Defence with the intention to use only the cockpit for some sort of sim. A company called GJD Aviation had

Ged plans on taking moulds from missiles on loan from a museum and will then recreate them using composites to complete the 'fully combat ready' look.

AV-8B Harrier 163423 wearing her 'Wake Island Avengers' markings taken at El Toru Air Show in April 1997. (Ed Groenendijk)

removed most of the cockpit and retained what was left, Ged then purchased it from GJD and had it transported to Everetts in Ipswich.

The McDonnell Douglas Harrier 2 was manufactured at the factory with an extensive use of carbon composites including the wings, cockpit, flaps, and control surfaces. Ged was in the perfect situation to take on this project as his day job involves designing and building the bodywork for World Championship sidecar racing. An expert in working with carbon composites and mould design, he soon turned his skills to making replacement parts for the aircraft. By the time Ged, Les and Chris got the Harrier home, unlike the Jaguar, she required much-needed attention to get her looking remotely

Work well underway on the Harrier with the wings now fixed into position and a new tail fin that Ged has made and fitted to the aircraft. The patches of grey show the replacement panels that have been made.

This photograph taken of the Harrier on arrival in 2018 clearly shows the amount of work that was required to restore her back to her former self.

Now sitting on her own undercarriage, the Harrier is really starting to take shape with a new coat of paint and squadron markings; note the missile pylons under the wing now in situ.

like her former self. A new tail fin, a nose cone, and a whole host of other items such as flaps and ailerons were required to get the aircraft looking recognisable again. Ged went about taking moulds from borrowed parts for the missing sections and was able to recreate them in composites working from his workshop at home.

Who needs sweeping views of the countryside when you have a Harrier parked outside?

A Boeing B-52 Stratofortress used for illustration purposes. This photograph was taken at RAF Fairford in July 2009. (Jim Darling)

5 STEVE
FROM KANSAS

With a striking range of over 8,000 miles, the Boeing B-52 Stratofortress is certainly an American long-range bomber. Known affectionately by the air and ground crews who worked on them as the BUFF (Big Ugly Fat F****r), the B-52 entered service in the 1950s and since then has played a key role in America's arsenal, seeing action in Vietnam, the Serbian conflict and the wars in Iraq and Afghanistan. With constant ongoing upgrades to the aircraft, it is widely acknowledged that the Stratofortress will continue to fly well into 2040. It has often been said in jest that when the USAF retire the younger supersonic B-1 and the stealthy B-2 bombers, the pilots who fly them to the boneyards will be flown back home in a B-52 Stratofortress.

When I was chatting to Steve about the possibility of including one of his projects for this book, he sent me a photograph that made me look twice. The B-52 holds a very special place in my heart. It was in primary school back in the early 1990s that I recall seeing countless heavily laden B-52s trundle into the Gloucestershire skies en route to Iraq. It was the first, and last time that I have witnessed first-hand, aircraft on operational combat duties. When I conceived the idea for this book, there was obviously a 'wish list' of aircraft that I would hope to have the opportunity to feature, but I had not dared to hope that a BUFF would ever be included.

Steve found the B-52 cockpit section in the outside storage at the Mid America Museum of Aviation and Transportation in Sioux City, Iowa on 20 February 2010. The aircraft had been subjected to the elements for some years and had not escaped the attention of vandals.

Steve's B-52 is the only privately owned B-52G simulator in the world. The sim was built by Boeing in an effort to win a USAF simulator contract. Boeing were unsuccessful in winning the contract so as a result the USAF never owned this simulator. By March 2011, the sim had been sitting outside in the weather for nearly five years. Steve was astounded and intrigued with the condition of her mechanical undercarriage. He needed to act quickly as she was in the process of being sold to a scrap dealer when he intervened and acquired this historic piece.

Steve's research concluded that the cockpit section was cut from an actual B-52D. The interior flight deck had been converted to a B-52G, and then made into a flight simulator. The practice of using a real aircraft cockpit to build a flight simulator is no longer an economical method by today's standards. Steve learnt that this particular simulator was designed and built by the Boeing company as an entrant bid for a USAF B-52G 6 simulator contract in which Boeing lost out to Singer LINK. The simulator floated around Boeing for a few years thereafter. The US Air Force officially retired the B-52G fleet in 1994 so Steve can only presume Boeing deemed the simulator as excess inventory around this timeline.

He brought the B-52 back to his home in Augusta, Kansas, which is only 15 miles from

On 23 April 2011, Steve acquired the simulator from the museum.

The radome that Steve acquired from a local golf course fits the simulator perfectly. In the background is a DC-8-62, formerly of the Flying Tigers, that Steve sold to a group from Brussels.

the former Boeing Wichita plant and manufacturing home of the B-52s. Fortunately for Steve, his location is situated among a vast pool of B-52 resources which enabled him to access some otherwise unattainable parts for the simulator. One of these was the radome that had been used as a lightning shelter by a local golf course which had recently closed.

Steve accelerated the restoration of the simulator because he wanted it to be part of the 60th/50th anniversaries of the 1952 first flight and 1962 last rollout. Consequently, in 2012 he was able to attend sim ceremonies for both Boeing Wichita and Barksdale AFB, the Headquarters for Global Strike Command.

The simulator looking fantastic in 2012 with her new paint job at the first flight and last rollout anniversary.

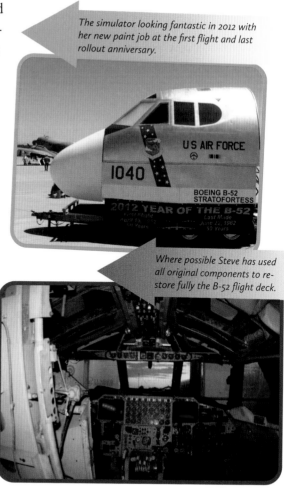

Ask anybody over the age of twenty-five what was the first aircraft that they ever flew on and the answer will more than likely be a Boeing 737. With over ten thousand 737s built, she is one of the world's most successful commercial passenger planes (second only until recently to the Airbus A320 family). Entering service with the German national carrier, Lufthansa in 1968,

Where possible Steve has used all original components to restore fully the B-52 flight deck.

Boeing 737-222 N9006U taken at San Francisco International Airport in August 1989. (Robert Poposki)

Boeing has constantly improved on the design over the years offering several different variants.

Steve's aim was to build a classic commercial airliner-style mobile cockpit with dual goals in mind. First, as a high-quality flight simulator experience, the second, as an active cockpit with lights and sounds that work for static exhibitions. In 2004 he purchased a stripped-out US Air 737-300 nose section and had it cut to fit a custom-built trailer. Then he had the nose section professionally painted in theme with a 1970s period United Airlines colour scheme. A complete cockpit interior that came from United Airlines 737-222 N9006U was meticulously installed. In 2010, the 737 mobile cockpit arrived at Nu-Tek AC instrument facilities in Augusta, Kansas and began the first round of integrations. By 2012, the project expanded with the addition of three computers and more interactive functions to help run simulated in-flight fire-warning systems, instruments, APU start and overhead functionality. What a project!

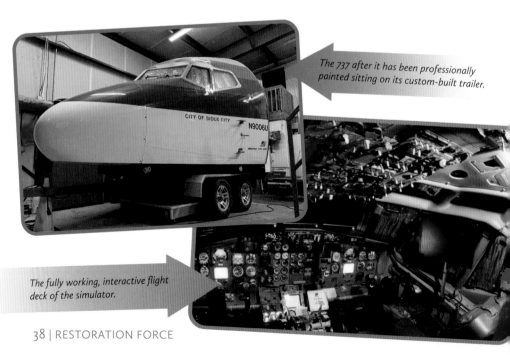

The 737 after it has been professionally painted sitting on its custom-built trailer.

The fully working, interactive flight deck of the simulator.

⑥ BOB
FROM ADELAIDE

Originally designed for the United States Navy, the McDonnell Douglas F-4 Phantom is a supersonic, twin-engine, two-seat jet interceptor/fighter bomber. Capable of flying twice the speed of sound and able to carry a wide array of modern weaponry, the Phantom not only became a firm favourite with the US Navy but was also used extensively by the US Marine Corps, the US Air Force and many air forces around the world. Entering service in 1960, the F-4 Phantom became a common feature in the skies over Vietnam serving with all three of the United States armed forces during the South East Asian conflict. The success rate was high, but so too were the losses with over 500 lost in action during the bloody war. With the introduction of the F-14 Tomcat and the F-15 Eagle, the Phantom was gradually phased out. The F-4 Phantom remains to this day the only aircraft to have been flown by both the Thunderbird and the Blue Angel display teams.

This stunning F-4J was built in November 1966 and entered service with the United States Navy Test Center under the registration 153768 until she was moth-balled in the late 1970s. After the Falklands War in 1982, the RAF permanently deployed 29 Squadron to the islands as an air defence against any further threat from Argentina, resulting in them needing to replace the squadron with Phantoms in the UK. In 1983, 74 Squadron was reformed

Bob's Phantom at his home in Australia finally mounted on its purpose-built trailer designed by him. She is wearing her original United States Navy colour scheme and registration 153768.

after the RAF purchased 15 moth-balled Phantoms from storage at Davis-Monthan Air Force Base in Tucson, Arizona having been upgraded to UK standards.

ZE350 was Wing Commander Graham Clark's aircraft, and differentiated from the other 14 Phantoms as she was the only one not fitted with the external upper-intake electronic pods usually seen on the 'J' and upgraded 'S' models.

The RAF had decommissioned most of their Phantoms by 1991 with most of them heading for the scrapyard due to the existing US government legislation, but ZE350 was saved from this fate as she was deployed as a ground target on a Welsh gunnery range, where she would remain up until the late 1990s. After her time at the Pembroke range, ZE350 was sold to a scrap merchant where she was purchased by a Welsh farmer who already owned a collection of old British aircraft. Due to its sheer size and to make transportation easier, the cockpit was separated from the main fuselage and the cockpit section was 90 per cent restored and placed into his private collection.

ZE350 in her original 74 Squadron paint scheme during her early restoration days.

When that collection was completely sold off during 2016-2017, Bob jumped at the once-in-a-lifetime opportunity to own such an iconic piece of aviation history. He purchased the Phantom and had it shipped to Adelaide to take on the challenge in order to show his respect to the designers, aircrew and ground crew who worked on this wonderful aircraft.

ZE350 taken at the Avalon Air Show in 2019. The F-35 pilots in the background held their position for over a minute to allow Bob to take this superb photograph.

Another superb photograph taken at the Avalon Air Show in 2019.

Left and below, inside the cockpit of Phantom ZE350.

7 HARRI
FROM SOUTH YORKSHIRE

Manufactured by de Havilland Canada, the 'Chippy' was a welcome replacement to the outdated de Havilland Tiger Moth biplane. Adopted by the Royal Air Force as its primary trainer, the two-seat monoplane entered service soon after the end of the Second World War. The Chipmunk was employed by the university air squadrons and enjoyed a long service in the RAF before the Bulldog started to replace her in the 1970s. Chipmunks were not completely retired as many air experience flights with the air cadets continued to fly the Chipmunks into the mid-1990s. Although not used for flying displays, two Chipmunks are still in service with the Battle of Britain Memorial Flight to train pilots in an aircraft that uses a tail-wheel 'taildragger', a design that is now no longer used in the current RAF fleet.

Harri was first introduced to Chipmunk WK638 back in the late 1980s. He was a member of the local air cadet squadron and his nearest RAF station, Finningley was just a few miles down the road. No. 9 Air Experience Flight (AEF) operated there and this is where he would go for some quality time cruising around the skies over Doncaster in the back seat of the venerable de Havilland trainer. On one day, flying was scrubbed due to inclement weather and to appease the eager flyers, they were led down to the hangar where the Chipmunks were kept to have a good look around at each of the

Harri's shed in his back garden. Harri had a wider door installed years previously so that the shed could accommodate a motorbike.

aeroplanes, 638 included. Perusing his flying log years later it turned out that WK638 was the only 9 AEF Chipmunk that he did not fly in, which in hindsight turned out to be quite unfortunate. His air cadet headquarters owned a Chipmunk cockpit, something he idolised.

So it was around this time he began to entertain the notion that one day he would own one.

Fast forward a few years to 1992 and Harri found himself working at RAF Finningley for Short Bros as an aircraft painter and finisher. Naturally, he was reacquainted with the 9 AEF fleet and carried out work on them from time to time. When the annual air show came around, one of his jobs was to make the static aircraft look pristine and in 1992 638 was chosen to represent the AEF.

Fast forward again, this time to the end of 2015. Checking through a well-known online auction site something jumped off the screen and took his breath away. The familiar red and white colour scheme and that unmistakable shape. Finally, after all those years here was the object of his desires! After a small bidding war and an incredibly generous gesture from sympathetic friends, 638 was his. He travelled the distance with trailer in tow to collect the cockpit and rear fuselage from none other than myself. He sensed that it was with a heavy heart that I bid farewell, but he knew that I realised she was going to a good home. With care and attention equal to bringing his first newborn home from hospital he drove back, and she arrived at her new abode, which ironically is one of the ex-RAF houses at Finningley. She truly had come full circle.

After doing a little digging, he discovered that her flying days had ended on 22 August 1999. As the aircraft was taking off from Bagby Airfield in North

A happy Harri and Chipmunk WK638 on arrival in South Yorkshire.

Yorkshire the left side of the engine cowling opened and flapped up slightly. The pilot noticed this but as he no longer had enough runway to stop safely, he continued with the take-off reducing power once he was airborne. The reduction in power combined with a turn to port prevented the cowling from flapping up. The aircraft circuited

Mission accomplished! Harri and Chipmunk WK638 looking extremely comfortable in her new home.

and began its approach to land, but at between five to ten feet above the east end of the runway the engine stalled and the left wing dropped striking the ground. Thankfully both passenger and pilot escaped serious injury but 638 was a write-off.

Luckily for Harri, the cockpit section fitted nicely into his garden shed, but only just. Years previously he had owned a motorbike and had had a wider door installed to the shed to cater for getting the bike through it. This proved essential for getting the cockpit in there. A year or so later, he traded the rear fuselage for quite a few components so that he could continue full steam ahead with the restoration. He was pretty sad to see her go but realistically he was never going to be able to store her anywhere undercover and the bits he obtained were ones he had been looking for (plus his good lady was never a fan of his small back garden looking like an aeroplane crash site). The rear fuselage ended up being delivered to a man at Harri's local aircraft museum. He had seen a post on Facebook and said it was something he could use. Harri dropped the fuselage off for him at the museum but doesn't think he used it on any of the museum exhibits, purely intending it for personal use. A big question on his mind was 'preservation or restoration?' He eventually figured that there would probably be rather a lot of fabricating of parts, plus taking into consideration the condition of some of the parts he had picked up, restoration would be the way to go.

He concentrated on the front cockpit initially and planned to get that completed before moving onto the back. There have been some compromises with some components that were not 100 per cent Chipmunk, but his aim is to replace these if the authentic parts turn up. There have been a few discussions regarding the rear cockpit and what to do with her. The obvious

It turns out Harri is not just an accomplished aircraft restorer. WK638 drawn by Harri.

thing for Harri to do is to restore her back to her original condition, but part of him would like to do something a little different. A Chipmunk flight simulator is a popular suggestion from his friends; Harri admits that this would be kind of cool and is giving it some serious thought.

The one question Harri gets asked more than any other is 'what are you going to do with her when she is finished?' Harri admits that he has not thought that far ahead. He concedes that she may never be totally completed as there is still so much to be done. He certainly cannot imagine getting rid of the cockpit after waiting nearly 30 years to own one. When discussing this subject with a close friend of his, his comment was 'sometimes the journey is more enjoyable than the destination'. Whatever happens, Harri can be satisfied that a little part of his history, RAF Finningley history and de Havilland history will live on in his humble garden shed (see below).

Opposite, above: Piper Aztec G-BBTJ taken in June 2009 at Wickenby Aerodrome. (Terry Fletcher)

8 JON
FROM LINCOLNSHIRE

The Piper Aztec is a light twin-engine aircraft that has been in production since the early 1960s. Her ability to compete with her closest rivals on three separate fronts, speed, baggage space and number of seats made the Aztec a popular choice with operators around the world, both in a civilian and military capacity.

Piper Aztec G-BBTJ was built in 1973 having entered service on 27 November of that year with Webster Aviation Ltd based at Leavesden Airport. She always remained on the British register (a rare things these days) having been acquired by seven other British firms before being purchased by Coopers Ariel Surveys Ltd, Wickenby in March 1995. Having been modified for aerial survey work her CV at this time already boasted sorties over Kuwait after the Iraqi invasion of 1991 surveying and monitoring the oil fuel line. She would serve with Coopers until 26 July

Locals in Ghana gather around G-BBTJ in 2008. (Jon and James Bryan)

G-BBTJ sat on the runway at Accra International Airport, Ghana in 2008. (Jon and James Bryan)

2010. After a long and colourful service, she was eventually withdrawn from use in 2013.

Jon's story is as interesting as it is heart-warming. He is one of only two people featured in this book who can say that they have worked with their aircraft during its operational life. Jon used to work for Coopers Aerial Surveys as an engineer and would fly to countless places with the Aztec. He fondly recalls the time when the aircraft was flying in Nigeria and the pilot had to set the plane to autopilot, jump in the back and get the RC8 camera running then sit on a modified bar stool (the legs cut down) in the P2 position to adjust the autopilot while operating the camera.

The list of countries that Jon can recall the aircraft visiting while on survey operations is vast, including France, Spain, Morocco, Algeria, Senegal, Mauritania, The Gambia, Côte d'Ivoire, Ghana, Nigeria and Finland.

G-BBTJ undergoes maintenance in the hangar while Jon tucks into a light lunch. Photo taken at Accra International Airport, Ghana in 2008. (Jon and James Bryan)

When Coopers decided to replace Aztec G-BBTJ they turned to Jon to dispose of her. "TJ was such a reliable aircraft that when I was asked to scrap it, I couldn't let her go that way, so offered her a home with me in the garden and so was gifted her." With Jon buying an old pub that had ceased trading, he found himself with the old car park which was a perfect place to keep his old friend.

The Aztec getting loaded and readied for her next flight at Accra International Airport in 2008. (Jon and James Bryan)

On her way home. G-BBTJ being towed by tractor to Jon's residence in Lincolnshire.

TJ at her final resting place in the former pub car park at Jon's house.

All that is missing from the Aztec's cockpit is the radio equipment, otherwise it is intact.

9 STEVEN
FROM MELBOURNE

Steven's love for Vampires started 40 years ago as a seven-year-old child getting driven around by his grandmother in the western suburb of Totten-ham, Victoria when they came across a Vampire fixed to a stand. At the time, he did not understand why he was so fascinated by the aircraft, but he was hooked! Little did he know that one day he would own that very aircraft, Vampire A79-824.

Thirty years later he had optimised his skill set having been a qualified mechanic, a carpenter and had restored a number of classic cars and prop-erties in Victoria. Now operating his own business, by chance he stumbled across a Vampire for sale on eBay. He thought long and hard, and even dreamt about purchasing the aircraft and restoring it with a view to hanging it above his car collection inside his man cave, but decided against the idea as he had a young family and couldn't justify buying a 'broken aeroplane'. As time went by, he never forgot that Vampire, and at times deeply regretted not submitting a bid. All this changed however when by chance he met 'Captain Dick' also known as Richard Winterburn, who was very well known in Australia for salvaging old aircraft from all around the country and trans-porting them home to his private aircraft museum. After some negotiating, the only surviving Australian-made Sea Vampire, A79-840 was his. A good job too as Richard that afternoon had sold a fully complete Vampire cockpit and was receiving good levels of interest in A79-840.

Steven's shed that he specifically built to house his Vampire.

After weeks of planning and building a bespoke shed to accommodate the aeroplane, Steven finally had the Vampire at home with him. At this stage, the airframe was about 70 per cent complete but it was missing all the cockpit instruments, bang seats, the Goblin engine and fuel tank. Thinking that it was going to take him years to gather all the parts, he concentrated on preserving what he had as he was expecting it to be an exceptionally long restoration. Unexpectedly, he received a phone call from Richard Winterburn. It turned out that the person who had bought the complete cockpit section from Richard no longer wanted her and so was subsequently offered to Steven. Without any hesitation Seven jumped at the chance and Vampire A79-660 was added to his collection.

The pod of 660 was not initially in the best of conditions as it had spent many years fixed to a stand. After ten years and 1,500 man hours spent on her, she was eventually restored. Steven's plan is to use this cockpit section as a donor ship for all the missing cockpit components for A79-840.

Opposite page: Vampire A79-660 on display outside the Channel 7 Studios at Tuart Hill in Perth, Western Australia taken in April 1984. (Peter Lea)

Below: Steven's second de Havilland Vampire, A79-660, that he plans on using as a donor aircraft for his other Vampire project.

Vampires 660 and 840 in Steven's garage.

Years passed and Steven was still on the hunt for more parts, but with Vampires having been made partly out of wood and most of them having been stored outside there were not really many left. One day however he was in luck as he happened to stumble across a piece of land that was being developed and which had Vampire A79-623 resting on it. It was Steven's if he could take her away, the only caveat being that he only had four days to remove her otherwise the bulldozers would bury her in the ground.

In those four days he made two trips to Sydney, some 825 kms away from his home. In addition, he also arranged for the wings to be transported by truck back to his home as he desperately needed the flaps for A79-840. The rest of the aircraft was to be loaded onto Steven's trailer for him to drive the Vampire back, thinking that the rear booms would come apart easily and he would be back on the road again in no time. This proved not to be the case.

With over 60 years out in the elements the booms were refusing to be parted. After a call to the road attorney in both states he was able to move the tail section by road having been just 30 mm under the maximum load limit. Spending 14 hours driving from Sydney to Melbourne taking up two lanes having lorries squeezing past is something that he would not like to do again!

When Steven returned home and his stress levels started to return to normal, he

Steven's third Vampire. A79-623 prior to removing her from the site.

Steven and Vampire A79-623 on their 14-hour journey from Sydney to Melbourne.

started to dismantle A79-623. To his amazement he soon discovered that A79-623 was actually A79-824, the very same Vampire that he had first laid eyes on as a child when he was being driven around by his grandmother.

Steven's grand master plan is to restore Vampire A79-840 to a high-quality complete static aircraft using missing components from A79-623 and A79-660. It is certainly a long-term project which he plans to do in his retirement, but his eventual goal is to have the finished aircraft in a museum so that she is preserved for future generations to enjoy.

Inside the cockpit of A79-660. She will donate her instruments and remaining parts to A79-840.

Vampire A79-840. Steven plans to restore her back to a complete static airframe.

Next page, first image: De Havilland Sea Venom WW145, a very similar aircraft to the subject aircraft featured in the chapter. Photograph taken at the National Museum of Flight in June 2010. (Peter Clarke)

10 PETER
FROM SOUTH MANCHESTER

Derived from the Venom night fighter, the Sea Venom entered service in 1954 and was designed to be carrier-based serving with the Royal Navy, the Royal Australian Navy, and the French navy. Differentiating from the Venom night fighters, the Sea Venoms evolved to have folding wings, an arrestor hook for carrier landings and a strengthened undercarriage. Soon after their introduction to service with the Royal Navy, the Sea Venoms were used in anger in 1956 to attack Egyptian targets during the Suez Crisis in the Middle East.

De Havilland Sea Venom FAW.22 XG692 cockpit section taken at her home in South Manchester.

XG692 was built by the de Havilland Aircraft Company at Chester, Cheshire in 1957 and survived two crash-landings before being delivered to the Royal Navy at the Royal Navy Air Station in Stretton. XG692 was issued to 891 Squadron in 1959 where she would embark on a round-the-world tour aboard HMS *Centaur*. She did not make it all the way to Australia as she was offloaded to RAF Seletar in Singapore before re-joining the ship on its way back to the United Kingdom. It was a journey that would see the Sea Venoms of 891 Squadron take part in Operation Damon which involved rocket attacks on rebels in Aden. Following the disbanding of 891 Squadron in 1961, XG692 was placed into storage at RNAS Abbotsinch until the end of the decade when she was issued to 750 Squadron at RNAS Lossiemouth to train Royal Navy observers. She was eventually retired in 1970 where she would end up at Royal Naval Air Yard Sydenham in Belfast in a disintegrating condition on the fire dump, until she was finally rescued in the 1980s.

Peter has now owned XG692 for over 23 years and during that time he has restored her from a wreck to what she is today. The cockpit is electrically live with all working lighting, functioning magnetic indicators and a working gunsight retraction mechanism.

The office! On the right-hand side of the photograph is the observer's radio panel and the AI MK21 air interception radar set beneath. The observer sits slightly behind and below the pilot.

The fully restored pilot's instrument panel.

Peter's Sea Venom makes a rare appearance outside at Newark Air Museum's Cockpitfest.

Hawker Sea Hawk WF144 in the foreground and Sea Hawks WF143 and WF145 in the background, taken in 1952. (Royal Aeronautical Society, National Aerospace Library/Mary Evans Picture Library)

11 ANDREW
FROM DEVON

When Andrew first got in touch to say that he had a number of projects in his collection that he was willing to share with me, I wasn't expecting to see anything like the levels of preservation that was being shown to me month after month. As the weeks passed, another section of aircraft would appear in my email inbox; I felt like an infant during Advent waiting for the next morning to arrive so that I could reveal the next chocolate treat in my calendar. Being quite the norm for a cockpit section to pass from one aviation enthusiast's hands to another, it is always something rather special to see rare aviation pieces being rescued and preserved from the scrapyard, and even more extraordinary, being trawled up from the sea off the coast of Malta as is the case of one of Andrew's pieces.

Hawker Sea Hawk F. MK1 WF145 was the third production Sea Hawk aircraft and was used in trials including landing and catapult trials aboard HMS *Eagle*. Her first flight was from Dunsfold in March 1952. Towards the end of April, she was with C Squadron at the Aircraft and Armament Experimental Establishment (a research facility for British military aircraft) carrying out arrested landing and catapulting trials. By the October of the same year, she was at Hawker Dunsfold going through performance trials. She would commence radio checks in February 1953 at the Royal Aircraft Establishment in Farnborough, before heading back to Dunsfold airfield in

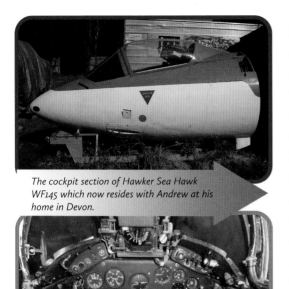

The cockpit section of Hawker Sea Hawk WF145 which now resides with Andrew at his home in Devon.

Inside the beautifully restored cockpit of Andrew's Sea Hawk.

March. She would do another stint back with C Squadron and then onto Armstrong Whitworth Bagington for modifications before arriving at RAE Farnborough in March 1955 for Green Salad radio trials (involving ultra-low-level flying to home onto a device on land). In August 1955 she was carrying out further catapult and arrestor trials at RAE Bedford before moving onto RNAY Fleetlands in February 1956 for an overhaul. She had spells at AHU Abbotsinch and Brawdy before she was finally struck off charge on 21 July 1959.

Next, Andrew turned his attention to Fairey Fireflies. The Firefly MK1 entered service with the British Fleet Air Arm in 1944 as a two-seat carrier-borne fighter/maritime reconnaissance aircraft. During the Second World War the Firefly was initially used for reconnaissance and anti-shipping strikes, but it was not long before the aircraft was being employed for ground-attack and anti-submarine patrol roles. The Firefly would go on to see combat during the Korean War, serving with both the British and Australian forces. Later variants of the

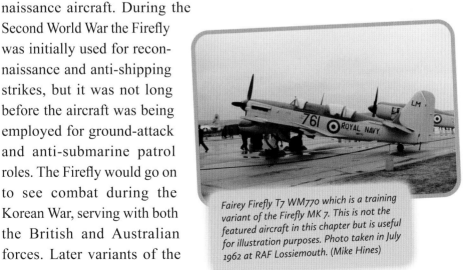

Fairey Firefly T7 WM770 which is a training variant of the Firefly MK 7. This is not the featured aircraft in this chapter but is useful for illustration purposes. Photo taken in July 1962 at RAF Lossiemouth. (Mike Hines)

Firefly MK7 cockpit creation using MK7 parts recovered originally from scrapyards.

There is no Fairey Firefly MK7 in existence, so this cockpit is the largest collection of MK7 parts anywhere.

Fairey Firefly AS6 WB271 again used for illustration purposes as Andrew's next project is a Firefly MK 6. This photograph was taken at Heathrow airport in 1973. (M. West)

Firefly would continue to operate in an anti-submarine role until it was eventually replaced by the Fairey Gannet in the mid-1950s.

The Firefly MK7 was heavily redesigned and is very different from the previous Firefly marks. Andrew's MK7 was created using many recovered parts from scrapyards, mainly Quarrywood in Elgin, Scotland, and he made a wooden frame so that the parts could be assembled together to make a cockpit.

Andrew's next project, Firefly MK 6 WD889, arrived at RDU Anthorn, Cumbria (Receipt and Dispatch Unit, which received aircraft from the man-ufacturer and modified them to service standards before dispatching them to operational squadrons) in January 1951. By the end of February, she was assigned to 814 Squadron. In October 1952, she nose-dropped while inverted at Lossiemouth causing minor damage to the aircraft. In November 1952 she was damaged again during a routine landing onboard HMS *Eagle* having bounced on the carrier's flight deck resulting in her undercarriage collapsing. By July 1953, she was at Royal Naval Aircraft Repair Yard (RNAY) Fleet-lands in Hampshire, for reconditioning where she would stay for little over a month before heading to Lee-on-Solent to join 771 Squadron X Flight. In December 1954, she was on free loan at Fairey Ringway before returning to RDU Anthorn in January 1956. In March 1957 she was sold as scrap and ended up in the Failsworth Scrapyard (Unimetal Ltd). She would pass through the hands of several museums including the North East Aircraft Museum and the RAF Millom Aviation & Military Museum before Andrew became her next custodian.

Andrew's collection is as diverse as it is interesting. His next item is the rear fuselage of Fairey Firefly VT409. VT409 was received by the RDU Culham in April 1948 before being dispatched to 810 Squadron at Lee-on-Solent in Hampshire. In July 1950, she was sent to Fairey Ringway for conversion to a AS.6. Having spent a couple of spells at RDU Anthorn and another short stint at Fairey Ringway in 1951, she was deployed to 820 Squadron at St Merryn in December 1951. She was sea bound in 1952, when in February of that year she bounced on landing resulting in the propeller pecking the deck onboard HMS *Indomitable*. In June, again onboard HMS *Indomitable*, her starboard wing tip hit the director abaft island. In October

Andrew's Firefly WD889 was constructed as a Firefly AS.6 which was an anti-submarine aircraft that carried British equipment. The AS.6 performed this role for the Fleet Air Arm until the mid-1950s.

Despite her first impressions, Firefly WD889 is overall very well preserved. You can see her main fuselage fuel tank and filler cap behind the pilot's position.

of 1952, she was loaned to 826 Squadron, before returning to 820 Squadron in November. By now she was onboard HMS *Theseus* where she was involved in another incident during night deck-landing practice when she floated into numbers 1 and 2 barriers. She was based at Kalafrana in Malta for a short period of time before returning to the UK, to Fairey Hamble for reconditioning in July 1953. In November 1953 she was back in Malta at AHU Hal Far before returning to the UK onboard HMS *Glory* in January 1955. In March 1957 she was sold for scrap.

As mentioned previously, there is always something special about a piece of historical significance being salvaged from the ocean. Andrew's next project is exactly that. Hawker Sea Fury VW589 was received at RDU Anthorn in November 1948. She had short stints in 1949 at AHU Abbotsinch, HMS *Unicorn*, AHU Hal Far, before she damaged a propeller on HMS *Glory* in January 1950. Four months later her fate would be sealed when landing on HMS *Glory*; the hook engaged Number 3 and 9 wires, but failed to arrest the aircraft which crashed over the port side, and she was struck off charge three days later. In 1989, the fuselage would see the light of day again when it was trawled up off the coast of Malta.

Above and below: The rear fuselage of Fairey Firefly VT409 where preservation is the order of day.

The rear fuselage of Sea Fury VW589, her RAF roundel is still clearly visible.

Last, but certainly not least is Andrew's final project, Fairey Firefly WB440. This Firefly was the last MK5 to be built, before it was converted to MK6 standard. She was converted to an AS.6 variant at Ringway in May 1950. She was at RDU Anthorn in February 1951 before being assigned to 826 Squadron in July 1951. She returned to the UK aboard HMS *Glory* in March 1954. In July 1954, she was at RNAY Fleetlands for reconditioning before returning to ADU Anthorn in October 1954. In the December of the same year, she was deployed to 737 Squadron based at RNAS Eglington before returning once again to RDU Anthorn in May 1955. In March 1957, she was sold as scrap. She would spend 23 years at Unimetal Ltd, before being put on display at Manchester Air and Space Museum where she would stay until 1987. When the aircraft left the museum, the cockpit went back to the owner and the engine was returned to the Fleet Air Arm Museum. For many years not much was done with the cockpit, but eventually she lost her home and was left outside which is when she seriously started to deteriorate. Thankfully, WB440 found its way into the custodianship of Andrew whose expertise and dedication will breathe new life into this Firefly.

VT409 and WD889 had come from the now defunct Millom Aviation & Military Museum but were not owned by the museum. WB440 came from Carlisle. VW589 came to the UK (possibly in the back of a Hercules) many years ago and became part of a Hawker Typhoon project/collection. It went through a couple of more owners before Andrew acquired her.

Fairey Firefly WB440 which is now Andrew's main project. He has enough parts to build a fuselage from propeller to tail, but even Andrew admits that this may take a few years before the task is finally completed.

Above and below: Andrew is going to incorporate the rear fuselage of VT409 (featured earlier in the chapter) and add a tail, engine, and propeller which he already has to complete the fuselage.

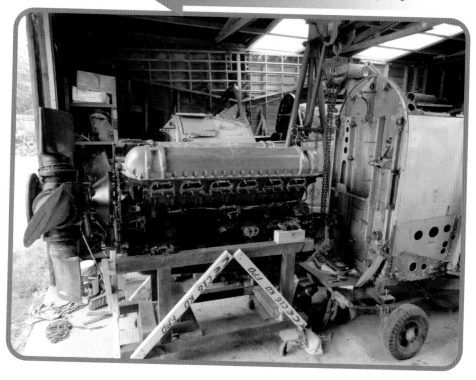

Hawker Hurricane PZ865 now flies with the Battle of Britain Memorial Flight. This photograph was taken at Farnborough in September 1962. (Tony Hancke)

12 TONY
FROM SOUTH WILTSHIRE

Tony started his collection, the Air Defence Collection, over 25 years ago to help focus his efforts in aviation preservation. With a particular interest in cockpit sections and the Battle of Britain, he set out on his long journey to restore items and artefacts for future generations to enjoy. Wherever possible, Tony uses original aircraft parts to assemble painstakingly each individual project ensuring that each item within his collection remains steeped in history and as authentic as it possibly can be.

Perhaps the best place to kick off with Tony's projects is his first and oldest project, Hurricane P3554. Tony is aiming for this to be a complete aircraft one day and currently uses over 85 per cent original Hurricane parts from the war. The project started in the 1980s with just a tailwheel. The identity, many cockpit parts and tubing all come from Hurricane P3554.

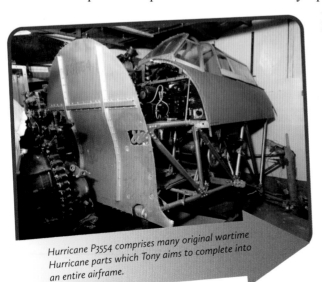

Hurricane P3554 comprises many original wartime Hurricane parts which Tony aims to complete into an entire airframe.

The Hurricane is a complex composite using parts from over 100 aircraft, many of them shot down during the Battle of Britain. All of the woodwork, cowlings and a handful of other parts came from the last-ever Hurricane to be built, Hurricane PZ865. These were removed from the aircraft in the 1980s when it underwent an extensive overhaul. Hurricane PZ865 is one of two Hurricanes that flies with the Battle of Britain Memorial Flight. In 2014, Tony was delighted when his Hurricane cockpit was used for the filming of the Scramble Experience at the wing building of the Battle of Britain Memorial.

The Hurricane cockpit being used during the filming for the Battle of Britain Memorial's Scramble Experience.

Tony's Hurricane on display.

Most of Tony's projects have a name, his second 'warbird' is called 'Bea' named after his grandmother who was the first wife of his grandfather. Tony's grandfather flew in the war and later went on to fly the Seafire F46 when he worked at the Directorate for Prevention of Accidents. The Seafire F46 was the Royal Navy's version of the Spitfire. Bea is built onto the remains of Seafire F46 LA546, using much of the cockpit structure.

Still remaining on the Second World War theme, we move across to a few more of Tony's projects. Utilising a Salisbury-built Spitfire windscreen unit, Tony decided to build what he calls a 'quarter cockpit' or desktop cockpit of a MK9 Spitfire. He used a Harvard grip fitted with an original brake lever post from a Spitfire. The electro gun button will allow Tony to add engine and gun effects.

A jump to the jet age now for Tony's next aircraft. Hawker Hunter F1 WT648 is one of two Hunter cockpits that Tony owns. WT648 is Tony's first jet cockpit section. When he acquired the Hunter in January 1991 the cockpit was in a sorry state having ended up in a skip. The windscreen had been buzz-sawed off, and someone had set fire to it and played noughts and crosses on its side with a buzz saw. Tony spent hundreds of hours in 1992 bringing her back to life.

The Spitfire MK9 quarter cockpit is an ideal size for Tony to exhibit at shows.

Seafire F46 dedicated to Tony's grandmother.

Meet Aurora. This is a Spitfire MK1 cockpit sliced through. Tony built Aurora to be 'access all areas' allowing people to be able to view inside a Spitfire cockpit. Once again, Tony used many original Spitfire parts to create this masterpiece.

Inside the cockpit of Tony's second Hawker Hunter, Hunter F2 WN890. This Hunter was a test aircraft most of her life and eventually ended up being scrapped and mostly buried. The cockpit was saved and used as an oxygen rig for test pilots.

Valerie is a Spitfire MK5 and is arguably one of Tony's most impressive projects. This section is from the firewall to frame 13 and Tony has managed to use over 65 per cent of original Spitfire parts.

Hawker Hunter WT648 after her restoration by Tony in 1992.

13 DAVID
FROM BELFAST

The Europa came in several variants and offered the private pilot low running costs, a competitive top-speed performance, a low fuel burn rate and an aircraft that was easy to transport and store. Sold in kit form, she was designed for the European market.

In 2015, G-TAGR was on a flight when the engine began misfiring. The pilot made two unsuccessful attempts to land at a nearby airstrip but on both occasions the aircraft had too much altitude and had to circuit the airfield. As the aircraft approached on the second circuit the engine cut out and the pilot was forced to make an emergency landing in a nearby ploughed field. The nose wheel dug into the ground causing such damage to the aircraft that she was deemed to be beyond repair.

David's career origins began in aviation working for a helicopter squadron, and then with the air ambulance in Belfast. He had always had an interest in anything to do with aviation, so when Christmas started to approach, he decided that he would give his son something of an alternative to a treehouse. The idea behind this unusual project was to get an old cockpit of any type and just mount it on a steel post. David purchased on eBay a 'stumpy 'cockpit section of a Europa two-seater aircraft which had the gullwing doors that he was looking for. Fortunately for David, his brother George, who lives across the road from him, is a good engineer and he conceived the idea of making the cockpit able to rise on a hydraulic ram from a tipping trailer, and then further decided that by mounting it on an old flywheel using a small 12v motor he could make it rotate as well.

Many long nights were spent in George's barn across the road welding, cutting and fabricating. David sourced all the parts while his brother welded the frame and fitted the swept wings. An instrument panel was fitted using old aviation dials and gauges and the cockpit was completed. A long nose cone was constructed before the process of testing began. Having passed 'pre-flight' checks with flying colours, the aircraft was sprayed, and NASA-related decals were added.

Opposite page: Europa G-TAGR at Stoke Golding Airfield taken in August 2010. (Terry Fletcher)

The cockpit section of Europa G-TAGR in David's brother's barn before the work began.

The final product. David's Europa looking most impressive in his back garden.

Opposite page: A North American T-2 Buckeye taken at Mississippi in 1974. (Steve Ryle)

'Apollo Eighteen' ready for flight. The NASA decals really add a professional finish to David's project.

The hydraulic ram in action really adds to the overall effect of David's spaceship.

The detail in the cockpit finishes off the project nicely.

The T-2 Buckeye is a subsonic intermediate jet trainer used to train Marine Corps and navy pilots. Capable of operating from the navy's aircraft carriers, the Buckeye was a relatively simple aircraft designed to be both forgiving and tough. The aircraft enjoyed a long career entering service in the late 1950s before she was eventually retired in the mid-2000s. The Venezuelan air force also employed the Buckeye, and although the United States Navy and the Venezuelan air force have retired their fleets of Buckeyes, the aircraft is still in active service with the Hellenic air force.

Featured in this chapter is a US Navy T-2C Buckeye operational flight trainer. These were a result of cooperation after trainers and researchers sat down together at Chief of Naval Education and Training (CNET) Headquarters to talk about the quality of navy training. Discussions focused on the future of computer-assisted instruction (CAI). Training time in aircraft was and is,

Denny and Sean's T-2C operational flight trainer. The cockpit is made up of actual cockpit components, some of which were modified for trainer use. They plan on integrating the switches, instrument indicators and such to turn it into a fully working flight simulator.

Sean who is partnering his father Denny with the simulator project, sat in the cockpit of the Buckeye that lives in their garage.

expensive in terms of fuel, man hours and sometimes lives. Too much emphasis was being placed on hardware and software without enough focus on the ultimate goal of training. The researchers' solution: "low-cost portable simulators that are simple, entertaining, and effective. They must be reliable for rough field usage and cheap for wide distribution."

Denny and his son Sean are no strangers when it comes to restoring cockpit sections. Denny started when he was only 11 years old back in 1966. He used a big cardboard box and made a space capsule. He cut the instrument panel out of cardboard, cut holes into it, and inserted used glass jar lids for recessed instruments. He then drew the face of the instruments on paper, cut them out and glued them into the lids. From that point on there was no looking back. From their home in Tampa, Florida, Denny and Sean have had a fair few cockpit projects in their time that include a BT-13 Valiant, an F-16, a PBY Catalina, and a CG-4 Hadrian. They currently also have their sights set on an F-1 Mirage cockpit that they plan also to convert into a flight simulator.

Denny was a USAF aircraft maintenance instructor, so his son Sean grew up in and around F-16s. His experiences as a young child moulded him to

Denny and a very young Sean taken back when Denny was serving with the USAF as an aircraft maintenance instructor.

be who he is today; this boy eats and breathes aviation. Their neighbours are quite used to peering into their back garden and seeing all kinds of fuselages, bombs, rockets, and so on. As well as cockpits, Denny restores Norden bombsights of which he has completed well over 100. In his own words, "we have to get old, but we don't have to grow up, we can still have our dreams".

The operational flight trainer is a perfect representation of the Buckeye's cockpit enabling training pilots to be completely familiar with the aircraft's instruments.

Denny and Sean's garage really is a man cave to be envious of!

One of Denny's previous projects. A Second World War BT-13 Valiant.

15 PAUL
FROM MELBOURNE

Jaguar XX977 was built in 1976 and delivered to 31 Squadron, Royal Air Force Germany. This was the only squadron that the aircraft served with, her code being DL. On 14 September 1984, during a low-level sortie the aircraft struck the Charwelton BT Tower near Daventry, Northamptonshire, ripping off approximately 5 ft from the port wing. The pilot sent out a Mayday and made an emergency landing at RAF Thurleigh in Bedford. The damaged caused was deemed to be beyond economical repair resulting in the aircraft never flying again. She went to function as an instructional airframe until eventually sold to Everett Aero in Ipswich. Paul purchased the cockpit section and had her exported to Australia in 2008.

If owning two fast-jet cockpits was not enough, Paul's third cockpit section is from what is arguably the most successful jet fighter family ever constructed. Approximately 12,000 MiG-21s were built and were used by over 70 countries throughout the world. MiG-21R serial number 1912 was a reconnaissance version of the famous MiG-21 Fishbed fighter built by Mikoyan-Gurevich at Gorky in the former USSR. 1912 was constructed in 1970 and was sold to the Polish air force. She served with the Poles in a variety of units until 2002 when she became surplus to requirements.

Jaguar XX977 taken in Kleine-Brogel Belgium in June 1976. (Alex Starvszkiewicz)

Opposite page: Paul's home in Melbourne, Australia which he shares with his wonderful wife Catherine. When he is not doing his day job as a train driver, his hobbies include wood working, rebuilding boat sheds, turning wine into urine and the odd bit of aircraft collecting.

Inside the cockpit of Paul's Jaguar XX977.

XX977 wearing her 31 Squadron markings in Paul's garage; the eagle-eyed reader will notice something rather exotic in the background of this photograph, the second of Paul's projects, a Sukhoi Su-22.

Sukhoi Su-22 4603 prior to take off as she winds up her engine for an engine test. Taken in Swidwin, Poland in 2001. (Joop de Groot)

Not surprisingly, information and photographs of the MiG's service behind the Iron Curtain are a little difficult to acquire. Sometime in the early 2000s the cockpit section was removed and transported to a private collection in Germany, from there she was sold and shipped to Australia in 2012. The cockpit section is painted in a highly unusual colour scheme that represents a unique Czech air force display aircraft.

Paul's Sukhoi is a Sukhoi Su-22 M4, serial number 4603 of the Polish air force. He bought the cockpit section from a surplus dealer called TDM Electronics in Poland. This is the first of two Polish air force cockpits that Paul owns.

Former Polish air force fighter 1912 painted to represent
a former Czech air force display aircraft taken at Avalon
Air Show in March 2017. (Derek Heley)

Paul's MiG-21 in his garage with the Su-22
behind it.

16 ANDREW
FROM ONTARIO

More commonly referred to as the T-33 or T-Bird, the Canadair CT-133 Silver Star is the Canadian version of the Lockheed P-80 Shooting Star sub-sonic jet trainer built under licence that was in service from the 1950s to 2005. It was the world's first purpose-built jet trainer in which several versions were produced for different roles such as photo-reconnaissance, armament training and pilot training.

Silver Star MK3 21631 started life in September 1958 when she was taken on strength by the Royal Canadian Air Force and flew with various advanced flying schools across western Canada. Nearly ten years later, in March 1967 she was transferred to the Royal Canadian Navy VU-32 Squadron, located in Shearwater, Nova Scotia where she would become a solo display aircraft, the 'Red

Andrew's former aerobatic display aircraft is a composite airframe built around 133631, seen here in May 2012 leaving O'Con Aircraft Supplies, Uxbridge, Canada.

Herring'. After the Canadian Armed Forces unification, she was assigned the new serial number 133631 in November 1970. In January 1975, 631 was transferred to ADMU Mountain View (long-term storage where she underwent controlled parts reclamation). She was eventually retired and struck off strength from the Canadian Air Force in October 1982. Just under a year later, the cockpit and fuselage remains were sold to O'Con Aircraft Supplies. Fast forward to April 2012 when Andrew was sold the cockpit and the remains of the fuselage as scrap material.

Andrew's interest in acquiring a cockpit started about 15 years ago when he acquired his first T-33 cockpit panel. Over the course of a number of years, he picked up a few more T-bird panels to add to the growing collection. A fellow aviation enthusiast suggested that he considered taking on a T-33 cockpit. Andrew reacquainted with another friend who would turn out to be instrumental in his quest to purchase a T-bird from O'Con Aircraft Supplies. After a few years of emails back and forth, a deal was put together. In April 2012 he picked out 631 as she was the most complete example in the collection, still retaining her original forward and rear cockpit panels, but needing all instrumentation, ejection seats, canopy, control sticks, exterior panels and lots of restoration and preservation. At the same time, he managed to purchase a tail section from another airframe with a vertical/horizontal stabiliser.

At the time of his purchase, Andrew had no idea that 631 was a significant historic aircraft. It all became very clear over the following few weeks, after information about her Royal Canadian Navy display career started to surface, that he had something very interesting on his hands. The cockpit still retains the 'smoke on/pull off' button on the front cockpit instrument panel from her display days as the Red Herring. Over the last seven years Andrew has acquired boxes of parts to aid in the reconstruction, and he is not yet even halfway through the project.

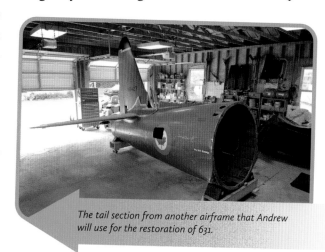

The tail section from another airframe that Andrew will use for the restoration of 631.

Opposite: A photograph of Percival Provost WE530 taken in 1951. She is not the subject aircraft of this chapter due to the fact that the aircraft featured herein crashed relatively early on in her service life resulting in very few available photographs. (Mike Dowsing Collection)

Silver Star 631 well on her way to being completely restored sitting on her custom-made cradle.

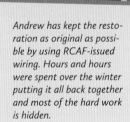

Andrew has kept the restoration as original as possible by using RCAF-issued wiring. Hours and hours were spent over the winter putting it all back together and most of the hard work is hidden.

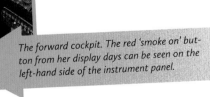

The forward cockpit. The red 'smoke on' button from her display days can be seen on the left-hand side of the instrument panel.

17 CHRIS
FROM SOMERSET

The Percival P.56 Provost is a single-engine, two-seat basic trainer which replaced the Percival Prentice. The P.56 entered service with the Royal Air Force in 1953 initially serving with the Central Flying School's Basic Training Squadron based at RAF South Cerney. In total 461 Percival Provosts were produced, 391 of those serving with the RAF until she was replaced by the more powerful Jet Provost. By the time the last-serving RAF aircraft was retired in 1969 the Percival Provost had been exported to numerous countries around the world including Iraq, Burma, Sudan and Oman.

Percival Provost WW453 was built in 1953 and served with 2 and 6 Flying Training Schools. After an accident in the 1950s at RAF Hullavington she was almost deemed to be beyond repair, however she was partially repaired and put into storage for a number of years. She was sold back to Percivals with a view to sell onto the Royal Air Force of Oman, a move that did not go ahead. Now surplus to requirements she was eventually sold to the Strathallan Aircraft Collection, then onto Kennet Aviation in Bedfordshire.

Chris from Somerset was aware of this Percival Provost ever since a very good friend of his bought it from Kennet Aviation, two decades ago. About 10 years ago his friend started to restore another Provost back to an airworthy status which left him not quite knowing what to do with his other Provost, WW453. Knowing that Chris had always wanted a cockpit or a static aircraft Paul, Chris's friend, decided to give her to him.

Chris leaning on Provost WW453 with his best friend Paul stood next to him. Percival Provost WW388 can be seen in the background. Paul is using this Provost as a spares aircraft to get his other Provost project airworthy.

Chris was an early post-war aviation archaeologist and has a special love for 1950s aviation. His ultimate goal is to own a MiG-15, 17 or 19 cockpit section to display at as many events as possible so that children young and old could sit in her to try and raise funds for UK charities. He is a preservationist in every sense of the word, aware that the majority of aircraft enthusiasts and restorers are an aging community. He is mindful that if we cannot introduce young blood and encourage the younger generations then so many museums and skills will be lost over the next few decades.

Although WW453 has been sat incomplete for years, Chris only needs a few parts to get her back to a complete airframe again such as the propeller hub and blades and the seats, which according to him are as hard to find as unicorn poo!

Chris set up a small display at Westonzoyland in Somerset to attract interest in Provost WW453.

Again, at Westonzoyland, Chris's stand displaying information and parts from WW453 including the flight panel.

The wings of WW453 ready to be fitted to the fuselage.

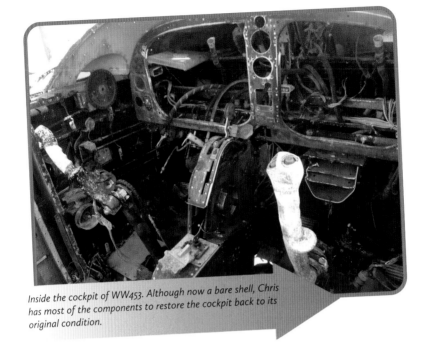

Inside the cockpit of WW453. Although now a bare shell, Chris has most of the components to restore the cockpit back to its original condition.

WW453 is currently painted in a yellow primer. When the aircraft was at Strathallan she was painted in a silver and blue civilian colour scheme. Chris aims eventually to paint her in her original RAF colour scheme.

18 JASON
FROM SOUTH WALES

The Gloster Meteor entered service with the Royal Air Force during the latter years of the Second World War and was the first Allied jet aircraft to fly in the war. Although the Meteor would see limited action during the Second World War, she would encounter more than her fair share of combat flying with 77 Squadron of the Royal Australian Air Force when she went head to head against the far superior MiG-15s. With the introduction of the more advanced Hawker Hunter and Gloster Javelin, the RAF started to phase out the Meteors in the late 1950s and early 1960s. However, Meteors played a significant role in the development of the Martin-Baker ejection seats, and the company still use a Meteor at their test facility in Chalgrove, Oxfordshire to carry out high-altitude ejection tests.

Meteor WL405 was issued to Bomber Command at RAF Hemswell in August 1952. In September 1954 she moved to RAF Wittering where she would spend two months before being shipped to 231 Operational Conversion Unit at RAF Merryfield. Having been deployed for communications duties at RAF Hemswell on 30 November 1956, she would remain there for four years until she was involved in a flying accident. After she was repaired in August 1960, she was placed into storage with 5 Maintenance Unit. She was then loaned to the Ministry of Aviation, Farnborough, in 1962 and moved to Martin-Baker for spares in 1987 where she would remain until

November 2001. She was next acquired by the Meteor Flight in Yatesbury where she was assessed for restoration. From there she would pass through the hands of several private enthusiasts before she was purchased by Jason.

Jason would not be the first person who purchased his cockpit on the internet whilst slightly intoxicated, and I am sure he will not be the last! What started off with intending to buy a nice car ended up in the ownership of a jet cockpit section. This is Jason's amazing story:

"Basically, it was a few weeks before my 50th birthday. I had moved back into my parents' house as they had passed away and I was in the middle of a divorce. I was feeling very sorry for myself. I had five beautiful children, four grandchildren by three different partners, three different mortgages over the years with two of my exes, three beautiful houses and here I was back in the bedroom I grew up in, sharing the house I grew up in with my sister who had decided to modernise it.

"She was away with work and I was off work for a few days and went on a diet of pasties and Strongbow. I had the intention of buying a nice Audi, but about two days into my one-man party I saw the aircraft advertised and went for it. I made an offer and the guy accepted it. It was on an open forum so I could not pull out as he is well respected and I would not let him down and pull out. My sister returned home and I informed her of what I had done. She thought I was insane and forbade me to use her garden! Then luckily for me I contacted Gary Spoors of the South Wales Aviation Museum and he agreed to let me use their hangar."

The ultimate aim is to restore WL405 to display standard so it can be exhibited at the museum.

On the day that Jason picked up the Meteor after driving for four hours, he got within 25 minutes of the museum when the clutch went on his hired Transit. After being towed off the motorway by Highway Patrol, he had a four-hour wait in the boiling hot sun for a recovery vehicle to arrive. When a big tow truck finally turned up the driver got out and asked, "what's that, a submarine?" Needless to say, Jason was not impressed. The cockpit spent the next three days on a ramp in a garage stuck on the back of the Transit.

The start of what would turn out to be a very long three days.

Opposite page: You never know what is hiding behind closed doors. Malcolm's barn in Staffordshire.

Mission accomplished! Jason's Meteor arrives at the South Wales Aviation Museum.

WL405 at her new home in Wales with her nose cone now fitted.

Jason has started collecting missing components for his cockpit and has visited other Meteor aircraft so that he can research what is needed to complete the restoration of WL405.

19 MALCOLM
FROM STAFFORDSHIRE

Some years ago, Malcolm went to buy some spares (non-Spitfire related) from a London cabbie who lived in Chelmsford. When he went to collect the spares, a cockpit section was sat in his garage. At the time she was not for sale, but Malcolm expressed an interest and sometime later received an email asking if he was still interested in purchasing her as the gentleman had to convert his garage into living accommodation. With no hesitation, Malcolm did the deal. When he went to collect the cockpit, he found to his pleasant surprise that the cabbie was also including the rest of the fuselage which had been cut off from the cockpit section. At that time Malcolm was unable to establish any of the aircraft's history.

Sometime later, when Malcolm went to purchase some aircraft spares for his project from a gentleman in Northampton, he discovered that this man had been the original maker of the replica and was able to supply Malcolm the photograph on page 90, top. Over the years it turned out that the Spitfire had been altered by various previous owners and was now in three pieces and part converted to a MK IX Spitfire. Malcolm set about acquiring a set of original MK II fittings and started the reversion back to that mark. There is still a long way to go, but a Lancaster project is currently taking priority, something hopefully Malcolm will share in the second edition of *Restoration Force*.

(CB-Aero of Northampton)

This replica Spitfire MK II is painted in the markings of 603 Squadron carrying the letters XT (603 Squadron) and D which denotes the individual code for the aircraft within that squadron. It was quite common practice that during the operational life of an aircraft the squadron letters would change as and when the aircraft got deployed to other units. One thing that would remain with the aircraft throughout her time in service was the serial number which was usually painted in black and located at the rear of the fuselage close to the tail section. Malcolm's Spitfire is currently painted with the serial number P7530. The original Spitfire P7530 was on a routine training exercise in 1943 with the Central Gunnery School based at RAF Sutton Bridge when it collided with an RAF Wellington bomber killing both crews.

Work progressing in converting the Spitfire back to a MK II.

Malcolm's completed blind-flying panel now ready to be fitted to the aircraft.

The starboard side of the Spitfire, the seat in the foreground.

Work on repairing the rear fuselage of the Spitfire has begun.

20 BEN
FROM SYDNEY

Derived from the market-leading Airbus A319, the A319 has a shorter fuse-lage than the A320 (shorter by seven fuselage frames) and is predominantly used for short- to medium-haul flights. Entering service in 1996, eight years after the introduction of the original A320, the A319 has the longest flying range in its category. In 2010, Airbus announced the new generation of the A320 family, the A320 neo (new engine option). The newer, more advanced A319 neo offers more efficient engines, an improved cabin and overall fuel savings of up to 15 per cent compared to the older generation Airbus and its closest rival, the Boeing 737.

In August 2017, Ben purchased a large collection of cockpit parts from Air Salvage International based at Cotswold Airport near Cirencester, Glouces-tershire. The aircraft that Ben chose was a SilkAir Airbus A319 which was being broken up at the airport. Having purchased the parts in August, they eventually arrived in Sydney in December 2017. Straight away Ben started to construct the simulator in his apartment, but he has had to be very creative in trying to fit everything in, with his laundry sharing the space of his winter garden and with the simulator. As of now, only the main instrument panel, co-pilot's seat and side consoles have been mounted but over the following few months he aims to get the windows and perhaps the overhead panel in place as well. The project takes some serious planning; his next two goals are to implement the panel backlighting and to set up the projectors. Ben recently acquired a co-pilot's seat, but he is still on the search for the pilot's seat. Unfortunately, seats remain expensive because the electronics inside are usually refurbished and sold back to the airlines. He has recently had quotes of $9,000 for a single seat!

Ben's apartment in Sydney. He is building his Airbus A319 simulator in his winter garden/laundry room which is located through these glass doors off his living room.

Opposite page: SilkAir Airbus A319 9V-SBD preparing for departure in Singapore, photo taken in June 2014. (Jim Revell)

Ben's Airbus flight simulator taken before the co-pilot's seat was fitted and before the projector screens were installed.

The co-pilot's chair now mounted and in position really makes a difference.

Ben's latest progress is simply staggering, considering this is housed in his laundry room at home.

21 MICHAEL
FROM SOUTH MANCHESTER

Designed to replace the ageing Gloster Meteor, the Hawker Hunter was the longest-serving jet-fighter aircraft of her time. Construction of the prototype began in the early 1950s and in 1952 the aircraft broke the sound barrier for the very first time. Employed as the Royal Air Force's primary fighter for a decade, it was not until the heavily armed, supersonic English Electric Lightning entered service in 1963 that the Hunter would take on a ground-attack role. She would operate in this guise for many years until eventually replaced by the Blackburn Buccaneer.

Michael's interesting project is the remains of ex-Royal Netherlands Air Force N-202. Built under licence by Fokker-Aviolanda, Amsterdam, she was registered as aircraft number 474 in October 1957. After 10 years serving with the Dutch 322 and 324 Squadrons, the aircraft was purchased by Hawker Siddeley Aviation and converted to a two-seat training aircraft for the Chilean air force. By 1974 the single-seat nose section had been acquired by Pinewood Studios. The cockpit section would appear in the James Bond film *The Man with The Golden Gun* playing the role of the Chinese fighter that was recovered onto the upturned *Queen Elizabeth* by MI6 in Hong Kong. In 1983, the Hunter nose section would make her second appearance in a 007 movie featuring in the film *Octopussy*. N-202 can be seen in the airfield attack scene at the start of the film where a number of aircraft are in view in the main hangar.

Hawker Hunter N-202 on the set of Octopussy at North Weald as a 'MiG-23' lookalike taken in 1983. (Dave Taylor)

After N-202 retired from the film industry, she was recovered from Pinewood Studios by Dave Taylor in 1995. Having spent four years with Dave, she would end up hanging on the wall in Route 66 nightclub in Torquay. In 2009 Michael acquired her and started his project of turning the Hunter nose section into a fully working flight simulator.

Michael constructed a frame so that the cockpit could sit on it allowing the ejector seat to be clipped into place. All of the controls are spring loaded to provide some feedback and are connected via computer to FSX allowing the Hunter to be 'flown'. The main instrument panel is now complete and populated with the real instruments which have been converted to be driven by stepper motors, the aim being to make a pseudo-realistic Hunter sim. Michael has made it all modular so that it can be moved; he hopes to be able to take it Cockpitfest in Newark at some time in the future.

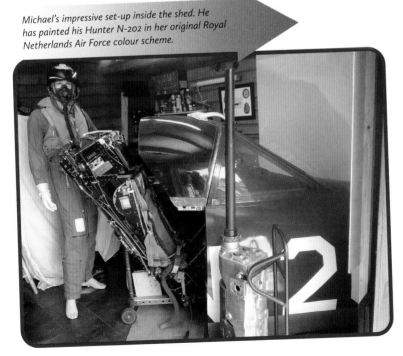

Michael's impressive set-up inside the shed. He has painted his Hunter N-202 in her original Royal Netherlands Air Force colour scheme.

Inside the Hunter cockpit which is fully lit with working instrumentation.

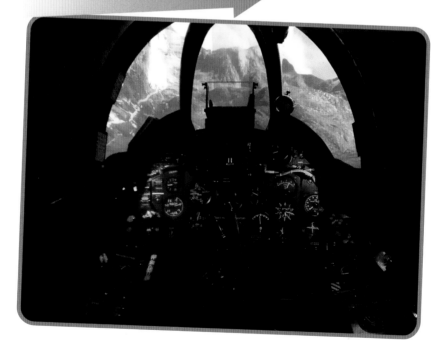

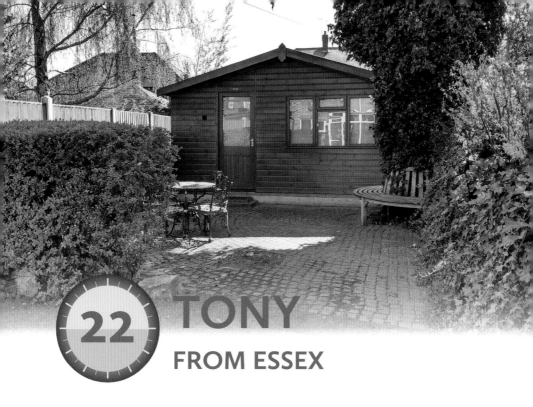

22 TONY
FROM ESSEX

When Tony contacted me asking if I thought his collection was suitable for this book, my first reaction was that it would not quite be the sort of material that I was looking to feature. I have had a number of approaches from kind people with instrument panels asking if their panel was suitable subject matter for the publication, and although each and every one was fascinating in its own right, there just wasn't enough 'meat on the bone' to fill an entire chapter. Then Tony sent me a photograph that literally made me go back to him begging for more!

Tony grew up near Southend (Rochford) Airport in Essex, so his interest in aviation started at an early age. He eventually went on to gain his private pilot's licence in 1988 and flew for fun for the next 12 years. In the late 1990s he decided that he wanted to collect a few analogue instruments, as analogue cockpits were disappearing fast. Like so many of us, he thought that digital cockpits are nowhere near as interesting as analogue when powered down. He considered the analogue instruments to be marvels of precision electromechanical engineering. He caught the bug, and "a few instruments" soon turned into a lot more.

Tony focussed on the Boeing 707 in the beginning because she was the first successful passenger jet credited with initiating the jet age in commercial

Opposite page: Anyone visiting Tony's garden in Essex would have no idea what is behind the door of his summer house.

Tony's Boeing 707, 727, E-6 Mercury and Carvair instrument panel collection.

travel. The 727 was the natural follow-on from the 707. The Boeing E-6 panels he stumbled across he couldn't resist, as they are so rare. She is also the final new derivative of the Boeing 707 to be built so rounds off the collection nicely. Tony then further added to his haul with the Carvair panel. This had sentimental value as the aircraft was designed and built by Freddie Laker's Aviation Traders Ltd at his local airport, and he clearly remembers them as a young lad coming and going.

The entire collection has taken 20 years to amass, and all the panels were acquired without instruments. After carrying out extensive research, Tony was able to source the correct instruments one by one, about 90 per cent being imported from the USA. All the panels on display here are in 'as flown' configuration and original condition, with a little conservation where required.

The forward panels of 707-321 are from Korean Airline HL7435 (ex-Pan Am N435PA) acquired from GJD Services Ltd in 2003. The throttle quadrant is from General Electric Aviation CFM-56 engine-test aircraft N707GE (ex-Pan Am N730PA). Imported from Arizona, USA, in 2005.

The Boeing 707-321 overhead panel is from Occidental Airlines Cargo EL-AKJ (ex-Pan Am N473PA). The panel was removed by Tony while the aircraft was being scrapped in 2007.

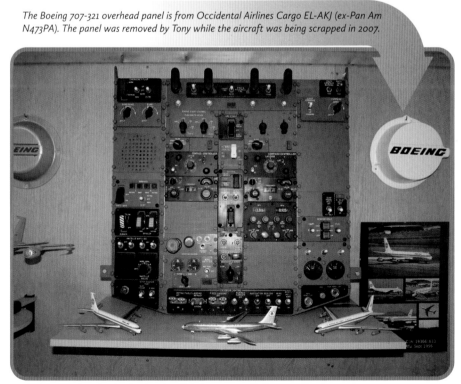

Above and below: Boeing 727-223 forward and overhead panels are from Air Contractors EI-HCB (ex-American Airlines N6817). The panels were bought from a collector in the UK in 2004.

Tony's attention to detail is evident in the restoration of these panels. It is as if they were removed from the cockpit yesterday.

Above: Boeing E-6 Mercury forward panels are from United States Navy 164409. The E-6 Mercury is still in service today with only 16 ever built. These panels were imported from the USA after the US Navy upgraded the cockpits to fully digital in 2006.

Aviation Traders ATL-98 Carvair captain's panel believed to be from British United G-ANYB (researched and confirmed by Carvair expert William Patrick Dean). Tony purchased this panel on eBay in 2006.

Opposite page, top: Geoff's garage in his garden in Kent. Most people keep junk in the loft of their garage, but not retired cabin crew Geoff.

British United Airways Aviation Traders ATL-98 Carvair G-ANYB taken at Coventry Airport in June 1964. (Martin Uzzell)

23 GEOFF
FROM KENT

In the introduction of this book, I wrote that I feared we were losing the romantic nostalgia that aviation once was, so it seems most fitting to end with Geoff from Kent, who was fortunate enough to have spent part of his adult life in the bygone era of aviation. He worked with BOAC/British Airways all of his career, mostly as cabin crew on types such as VC-10, DC10, Tristar, and Boeing 707, 747, 757, 767, and 777. Although he is now retired, he still regularly maintains his pilot's licence, mostly flying microlights.

The British Aircraft Corporation One-Eleven, or BAC1-11, was a short-haul jet airliner entering service with British United Airways in 1965. The One-Eleven quickly became one of the most successful British airliners, with many international

BAC Super 1-11s G-AVMX and G-AVMZ at Manchester Airport in June 1986.

airlines adding their name to the BAC order book. With a passenger capacity of 79, it was not long before the Super One-Eleven (or Series 500) entered service. Its stretched fuselage increased the passenger capacity to 119, offering airlines and the new package holiday operators even more cost effectiveness. The aircraft started to be phased out with the majority of its operators in the late 1980s and early 1990s, mainly down to new aircraft noise restrictions that were brought into many European countries.

Geoff has spent the last couple of years rebuilding his unique, ex-British Airways BAC 1-11 1960s airliner cockpit in the loft above his garage. The fittings are unashamedly analogue, with a vast number of levers, knobs, and dials. The beauty of this cockpit is that it is modular, so there is nothing that will not fit through a standard door in a house. Only the large GRP roof panel might need to be cut due to its size, so any average-sized room would accommodate this cockpit.

This was a British Airways (formerly BEA) BAC 1-11 510ED simulator, from which Geoff bought the virtually intact internal cockpit fittings from eBay a few years ago in disassembled form. There was a Dymo tape stuck on the roof lining with the registration G-AVMQ (in sequence with all the other BA aircraft) so whether it was the official or unofficial registration, Geoff has adopted it anyway! He has spent literally hundreds of hours completely disassembling all of the instruments, controls and panels and then

Geoff's very rare British Airways BAC 1-11 510ED simulator at home in his garage loft.

With only a small number of components to find, the main instrument panel is almost complete.

he meticulously cleaned, repaired, and replaced missing parts, adding plac-
ards etc. He had to fabricate the emergency evacuation alarm panel, and
although it looks very good, he is always on the lookout for the genuine
article (please do get in touch with us if you know of one going spare). There
was never a clock in any of the photographs that Geoff studied, as these
usually got 'misappropriated' so he fitted a blanking plate until he can find
a replacement. The nose wheel steering handles were also missing.

Geoff has not mounted the overhead engine instrument panel (which is
100 per cent complete) as it is too heavy for his current location. He still
has most of the GRP fittings for the ceiling, side units, and windows that
with some ingenuity and fettling you would be able to fashion a virtually
complete cockpit.

*Two BAC1-11s 510s at London
Heathrow taken in 1986.*

The overhead engine instrument panel which is 100 per cent complete but not yet fitted.

There is one square panel missing from the ceiling, but Geoff has all the drop-down emergency oxygen mask modules.

What better way to end than a photograph of Geoff taken at Blantyre Chileka Airport, Malawi in February 1982. He is stood in front of a SVC-10 that had just arrived from London.

INDEX